Voyager Passport F

Fluency
5

ISBN 978-1-4168-0669-1

Copyright 2008 by Voyager Expanded Learning, L.P.

All rights reserved. No part of this publication may be reproduced or transmitted in any form or by any means, electronic or mechanical, including photocopy, recording, or any information storage and retrieval system, without permission in writing from the publisher.

Printed in the United States of America   08 09 10 11 12 13   DIG   9 8 7 6 5 4 3 2

Table of Contents

Building Character
- Politeness: It Costs Nothing but Buys Everything 1
- The Qualities of Good Leaders 2
- Joey Takes a Stand 3
- Honesty's the Best Policy 4
- Cooperation: Drawing on Help from Others 5

Space Exploration
- LearnAboutSpace.com 6
- Solar Winds Blow Past Earth 7
- Who's That on the Moon? 8
- Are Spheres a Sign That Life Once Existed on Mars? 9
- Big Bear Observatory 10

How Do They Do That?
- How Do Wicks Get into Candles? 11
- How Cordless Telephones Work 12
- How Thermometers Work 13
- Check Out What Happened to Mom's Check! 14
- Recycling Helps Landfills Work 15

Exciting Games
- Let's Get Together 16
- Flying High 17
- Taking a Risk 18
- Freeskiing 19
- Extreme Sports and the Winter X Games 20

- Timed Passage 21
- Timed Passage 22
- Word List 23

Fluency Practice

 Read the story to each other.

 Read the story on your own.

 Read the story to your partner again. Try to read the story even better.

 Questions? Ask your partner two questions about the story. Tell each other about the story you just read.

Timed Reading

1. When you do a timed reading with your partner, make sure that you have practiced your story and know all the words.

2. When you are ready, tell your partner to start the timer.

3. Read carefully, and your partner will stop you at 1 minute. When you stop, mark your place.

4. Count the total number of words you read.

5. In the back of your Student Book, write the number of words you read and color in the squares on your Fluency Chart.

6. Now switch with your partner.

Politeness: It Costs Nothing but Buys Everything

Some people say, "Manners are caught, not taught." This means that people learn manners by watching what others do. They do not learn them as easily by listening to what people say to do.

Manners came about for different reasons. For example, do you know why people shake hands? Long ago, it was a way to see if the person you were greeting was a friend or an enemy. Of course, that is not really the case today. People shake hands because they know it is polite to do so.

Manners are a way of showing respect. By acting respectfully, people avoid problems. (103) They take turns speaking and don't interrupt others. At the table, they make sure others are not bothered by their actions. They knock before opening a door. They always remember to say "please" and "thank you."

Do you like it when people show you respect? If so, you have learned through experience why manners are important. Without them, many events could get out of control in a short time.

Try to remember as you go through your day that you will have many chances to use good manners. With any luck, others will learn from watching you. Then, good manners will continue to be passed along to make the world a nicer place in which to live. (220)

> **PASSAGE 2**

BUILDING CHARACTER

The Qualities of Good Leaders

What is a leader? Usually, a leader is the person responsible for a group's success or failure. In a football game, for example, the quarterback is the leader. He is in control, and he calls the plays. Without a good quarterback, a team doesn't play well.

Leaders are found in schools, in business, and in government. In fact, leaders are everywhere you look. Have you been to the grocery store lately? One person is in charge there. He or she is the manager. The store manager's job is to keep the store running smoothly. This is done by building a winning team of workers. This team does not need a leader with great athletic ability. Rather, it needs a leader with strong people skills and good work practices. (128)

Perhaps the most important leadership quality is the ability to gain the respect of others. People will not do well with a leader they do not respect. Gradually, they will become unhappy. The group will become weak and even may fail.

Why do you vote for certain leaders at school? Would you like to become a leader yourself? Whether you are choosing a leader or working to become one, here are some things that you should consider.

- Great leaders are trustworthy. They do what they say.
- Great leaders are honest. They always tell the truth.
- Great leaders avoid losing focus. They keep team members busy with the task at hand. (238)

Trustworthy

Honest

Focused

2

BUILDING CHARACTER

PASSAGE 3

Joey Takes a Stand

Joey was uncertain about the school in his new town because it seemed just the opposite of the friendly one he'd left behind. Back home, he would go outside with everyone at recess and kick the ball around. Here, it was too cold to go outside, so students just stood around in the gym.

To make matters worse, two older boys started picking on him at lunchtime. Joey tried to avoid them, but the bullies always knew where to find him.

"This is a disgrace," Joey thought to himself. "I can't allow these guys to keep bullying me, and I refuse to continue to suffer because of them!" (108)

The next day, Joey was sitting in the gym bleachers when the two bullies marched toward him.

Joey stood up, trying to control his fear, and said, "I will not allow you to bully me anymore. I might be new here, but that doesn't give you the right to treat me badly. It's time for you to stop, right now!" Then, Joey turned and walked away.

The next day at recess, a boy sat down next to Joey.

"That was awesome how you stood up to those bullies yesterday," he said. "I just moved here last month, and they tried the same thing on me. Maybe, between the two of us, we've taught them some manners!"

A smile gradually spread across Joey's face as he agreed with his new friend. (238)

Honesty's the Best Policy

Once there was a boy who was responsible for watching a herd of sheep near his village. This was a boring job, so to amuse himself, the boy cried out, "A wolf is chasing the sheep!" The villagers ran to help the boy chase the wolf away. When they saw there was no wolf, they felt angry at being tricked.

The villagers grumbled among themselves as they trampled back home. During the next few weeks, the boy repeated his naughty prank several times. Each time, the villagers got angrier and angrier. One day the boy saw a real wolf prowling around his flock. He called out loudly for help, but no one came. He cried even louder. Still there was no response. As evening came, the villagers went to look for the boy, who had not returned home. They found him weeping and looking for the scattered sheep.

This story teaches a valuable lesson about the importance of telling the truth. Must people always tell the truth? Sometimes people will tell a lie to protect a friend's feelings. Many people believe that as long as the reason for the lie is good, the lie itself is not so bad. On the whole, it is best to be honest at all times. People who do this are respected by others. They also feel good about themselves.

BUILDING CHARACTER

PASSAGE 5

Cooperation: Drawing on Help from Others

Two heads are better than one. This old saying means that people are more likely to find success when they work together. Think about your own experiences. Then, think about achievements you've read about. You're likely to agree that this saying rings true.

People always have worked together for common goals. Some goals are held by all people. Finding cures for diseases is an example of this kind of goal. Other goals, such as raising money for a park, are more local. Parents can share the goal of teaching table manners to their toddler. Clearly, goals can be large or small. ⁽¹⁰¹⁾ By working together though, people can make a difference. They can do things they might have trouble doing alone.

The students of Pleasant Valley School understood this idea. They wanted to paint one wall of their building. Someone suggested painting a mural. Murals are large works of art. It would take one person a long time to paint one. All of the classes pitched in though. Art teachers and parents helped too. They created a colorful mural. The design showed different school activities. In years to come, new students will see the mural. They will have a fine example of what people working together can do. ⁽²⁰⁷⁾

PASSAGE 1

SPACE EXPLORATION

LearnAboutSpace—for children of all ages who love to learn about space

http://learnaboutspace.com

Imagination Knowledge Exploration Discovery News

LearnAboutSpace.com

Find: [   ] Search

This Web site is designed for children of all ages who love learning about space. Simply click on a link that interests you and start exploring!

Solar System

Click here to learn about the nine planets in our solar system. Discover which planets are closest to the sun. Find out how much you would weigh on Mercury, and learn why some scientists think that Pluto really is a comet.

Deep Space

Click here to learn about objects deep in space. Learn how black holes use gravity to pull things toward them. Learn the difference between stars called Blue Giants and stars called Red Dwarfs. (104)

Telescopes

Click here to find out about the largest and most powerful telescopes on Earth. Then, read about the Hubble Space Telescope project. The Hubble telescope orbits above Earth and sends back stunning views of our universe. Discover how this telescope has changed our understanding of the world.

Space Dictionary

If your mission is to write a paper about space, this link will help you look up the words you need to use. The entries include diagrams, drawings, and even videos.

Our Night Sky

Click here to learn about the fabulous sights you might see in the sky tonight! (203)

SPACE EXPLORATION

PASSAGE 2

Solar Winds Blow Past Earth

A few years ago, science experts warned that some people might have problems with their TV and phone services. They explained that the trouble would be caused by a huge explosion on the sun. Luckily, the trouble never happened. Yet, it is true that explosions on the sun, called solar flares, can affect Earth.

Solar flares are giant explosions on the sun's surface. They occur in places where the sun's energy is very strong. The flares send brilliant blasts of gas and energy into space. These blasts, called solar wind, blow through the solar system. (95)

Problems can occur when energy from solar wind reaches Earth. Satellites can be harmed. Solar winds also can cause power failures and problems with cell phones.

Luckily, a magnetic field surrounds Earth. This is what causes compass needles to point north. It acts as a strong shield against solar winds. However, sometimes a small amount of the energy from a solar wind makes it through Earth's atmosphere. This usually happens near the North or South Poles. When this happens, people see the Northern or Southern Lights. These beautiful lights look like red, green, and pink clouds in the night sky. (195)

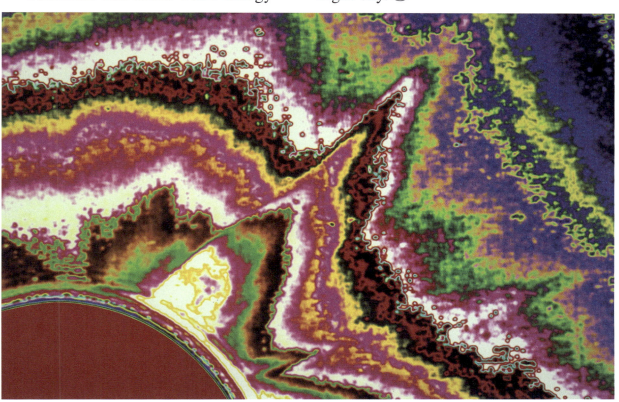

7

Who's That on the Moon?

Cameron frowned at his sister Hannah. "How can you say that there isn't life anywhere else except on Earth?" he asked. "The universe is so enormous that it would be impossible for you to even know."

"That's just what I believe!" Hannah said angrily, walking out of the room.

That night, as he drifted off to sleep, Cameron thought about his conversation with Hannah. Before he knew it, he found himself standing on the moon, getting ready to take a swing at a golf ball. When he hit the ball, it shot into the air and kept going, curving over the horizon until it was out of sight.

"Wow!" said Cameron. "I've never hit a ball that distance. I guess I forgot there's less gravity on the moon."

About that time, he heard a voice say, "Hello, Cameron." Cameron turned to see a small green creature standing nearby. The creature was about 3 feet tall and had red antennae and webbed feet.

"I must congratulate you on your swing, comrade," the creature said. "I'll bet the ball landed somewhere on the other side of Robert's crater."

"Thanks," Cameron replied.

Cameron scratched his head. "That creature's voice sounds just like someone I know," he thought. "I know I've heard it before, but I don't know where."

All at once, Cameron began to shake, or that is, something caused him to shake. He looked up to discover Hannah standing over him. "Cameron, get up and come to breakfast!" she said.

SPACE EXPLORATION

PASSAGE 4

February 20, 2004   Science Section   *Discovery Times* 24C

Are Spheres a Sign That Life Once Existed on Mars?

by Saturn Rings   Senior Science Editor

A few weeks ago, a rover named *Opportunity* landed on the surface of Mars. It has since been busy at work. Scientists are excited about its thrilling mission to explore a remarkable planet.

The rover has two cameras. After it landed, people working on the project used the cameras to look at the planet's soil. They saw small grains of sand and larger objects that looked like gravel. They observed that some of these larger objects were perfect spheres. About the size of tiny peas, the spheres caught their attention. The scientists wanted to see if the spheres also were below the surface of the planet. (106)

To do this, they got the rover to spin its wheels in the soil and dig a trench. Then it took pictures of the wall of the trench. These images showed that there were, indeed, more spheres. To the scientists' surprise, the spheres in the trench were shiny.

Science experts wonder what caused the spheres to form. Some think that the spheres were the result of a volcano. Others think they were formed by the action of water flowing through rock.

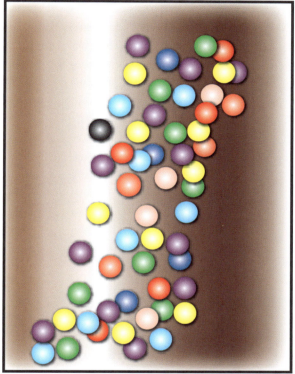

Courtesy of NASA

Some even think that they may have formed when a large rock crashed into Mars.

Many people are especially excited by one of these ideas. If the spheres were formed by water, it may mean that there was some form of life on Mars at one time. (234)

9

PASSAGE 5

SPACE EXPLORATION

Big Bear Observatory

A small, white observatory rises from the middle of a clear, blue lake in California. The building has the unusual name of Big Bear. From the outside, it looks quiet and grand. But inside, busy scientists are hard at work. Their mission is to learn as much as possible about Earth. They study subjects such as stars, gravity, and the solar system.

They are especially excited about one project. They want to find out why Earth has slowly gotten warmer. One reason may be that more sunlight is reaching Earth today than in the past. Another reason has to do with certain gases, such as those that come from cars. Scientists think that these gases may trap sunlight, causing the atmosphere to become warmer. (124)

Even though they are studying the sun, the scientists at Big Bear work at night, and they point their telescopes at the moon rather than the sun. They look at light called earthshine, which is the sunlight reflected by Earth. What does earthshine look like?

Think of a half-moon on a dark night, with one brilliant side and one dim side. Even though the dim side is dark, it still reflects some light. This light is earthshine.

Scientists at Big Bear do not know why Earth has gotten warmer. Yet they are beginning to gather facts. For instance, they know that the amount of earthshine changes from season to season. Over time, they hope to have an answer some day. (245)

10

HOW DO THEY DO THAT?

PASSAGE 1

How Do Wicks Get into Candles?

Long ago before there were electric lights, people relied on candles for light. For them, making candles was necessary. Today, most people make and use candles for pleasure. They enjoy the soft, flickering light, and the candles often provide a nice scent as well.

In its basic form, a candle is a simple thing. It is a column of wax surrounding a wick. The wick is just a piece of cord. Have you ever wondered how this thin, droopy material gets into the hard candle wax? Read on to find out, and you'll learn how you can make your own candle as well. (103)

Steps for Making a Candle

1. Put wax in a tin can, place the can in a pot of water, and heat the water until the wax melts.
2. Take another can, and tape one end of the wick to the bottom of the inside of the can. Line the inside of the can with a thin coat of oil. Place a pencil across the top of the can, and tie the other end of the wick around the pencil.
3. Shield your hands from the hot wax by putting on oven gloves. Pour the melted wax into the prepared can.
4. Allow the wax to harden for several hours. Then, remove the pencil, cut the wick to the right length, and slide the candle from the can. Enjoy relaxing by the light of your own homemade candle. (241)

11

How Cordless Telephones Work

It's a problem of modern life. You can't locate the telephone. It's not where it's supposed to be. In the old days, that never would have been a problem. The phone was always in its place, firmly connected to the wall by a wire. Today, cordless phones allow people to walk around while they talk. It's a convenience many people have come to enjoy. But, phones sometimes wind up in unexpected places.

The first cordless phones were large and expensive. Today, they are easier to own and use. Some even are made of waterproof materials to use at the beach or pool.

A cordless phone has two parts—a base and a handset. It is more than just a phone. It also is a kind of radio.

Here is how it works. (132)
- The base receives an incoming call. It changes the electrical signal to a radio signal, which it then broadcasts.
- The handset receives the radio signal and changes it to an electrical one. Then, that signal goes to a speaker. You hear the signal as words spoken, for example, by your grandmother.
- When you talk into the handset, your voice is changed to a second radio signal. This signal is sent back to the base.
- The base receives the radio signal, changes it into an electrical one, then sends it through the line. That is how the other person hears your voice. (233)

How Thermometers Work

Thermometers provide a service to people in almost all areas of life. They support the work of air conditioners and heaters. They are in refrigerators. They often hang in backyards to show how hot or cold it is outside. A thermometer is probably in your family's medicine chest right now.

There are several different kinds of thermometers. One kind is a small glass tube that surrounds and shields a liquid material. Numbers are printed on the side of the tube. When the liquid gets hot, it becomes larger in volume. There is no place for it to go inside the tube except up. When the liquid cools, it moves back down in the tube. The number next to the top of the liquid shows how hot or cold the liquid is.

Another kind of thermometer is the round kind you hang on a wall. A spring is used to measure the temperature in this kind of thermometer. A pointer is hooked to the spring. When the spring warms up, it gets larger. Then, it pushes the pointer toward higher numbers. The opposite happens when the air cools.

The newest thermometers work in yet a different way. They are electronic. A doctor might gently place one in your ear. He or she can tell in an instant if you are sick. The numbers pop up right away. These tools can cost a lot of money. If you are willing to wait just a minute or two, the old-fashioned thermometers still work just fine.

Check Out What Happened to Mom's Check!

Josie really wanted a new bike. Her mom offered to pay for half the bike if Josie earned the rest by doing chores. During the summer, Josie walked dogs, mowed lawns, and helped with young children in her neighborhood. By August, she had earned her half of the money.

On Saturday morning, Josie and her mom went to the bike shop. Josie picked out a bright red bike and a helmet to shield her head. She gave her cash to the salesperson, and her mother wrote a check for the difference.

On the way home, Josie asked her mom, "Why does your check work the same as my cash? How does the store turn your check into money?"

Josie's mom carefully explained. "First, the bike store deposits the check in its bank account at First Bank. Next, First Bank prints the amount of the check in the bottom corner. They use special magnetic ink. Numbers that show my bank and account number already are printed on the bottom of the check. Then, First Bank sends the check to a processing center. The processing center puts the check through a machine that reads the magnetic numbers. Using this information, they add the amount of the check to the bike shop's account at First Bank. They also subtract the amount that is on the check from my account at State Bank."

"While all of this is going on," Josie claimed, "I'll be having fun riding my brand new bike!"

Recycling Helps Landfills Work

When you finish munching on a sack of nuts, what do you do with the sack? What do you do with the plastic your sandwich is wrapped in? The average American throws away more than 4 pounds of trash every day. That's almost 30 pounds a week!

Most people enjoy the convenience of having their trash picked up at the curb or in the alley. Few think about what happens to it after that. After trash is picked up, it's taken to a landfill. Trained workers design landfills. They build them with the intent to protect the areas surrounding them. They place a liner at the bottom of the landfill. Then, workers add soil over the trash as needed.

Building a landfill can be a long and expensive job. First, a large area must be located. Then, the location must pass a study about how the landfill will affect the area. Once all of this is done, permits have to be granted. Permits must come from local, state, and federal levels. A short time ago, a new landfill was built in North Carolina. It cost nearly $25 million just to get it started.

One-third of the garbage in landfills is paper. Another third is plastic and glass. That adds up to two-thirds of all trash. These materials often can be recycled. It's something for people to think about as they create their share of trash each day.

PASSAGE 1

EXCITING GAMES

Let's Get Together

Folders [Add]

- Inbox
- Outbox
- Sent
- Draft
- Bulk
- Trash

To: Luisa

CC:

Subject: Let's get together

Dear Luisa,

I still can't believe that you live in another city. Every morning I expect to see you sitting in the front row of Ms. Gonzales's math class. Everyone misses you a lot.

I'm sending this e-mail to tell you about some exciting news. The Summer Extreme Games will be in your city the first week of August, and I'm coming with my parents to see them! We'd like to invite you to attend a few events with us. Here's a list of what's available:

- aggressive in-line skating
- stunt bike riding
- wakeboarding
- skateboarding
- motocross
- surfing

All these events would be so great to see. (106) However, we won't be able to see all of them, so let me know your favorites.

Meanwhile, my ability on my stunt bike has improved a lot. Maybe next year I'll be able to compete too. Today, I will attempt a 360 tail whip, which is a difficult move. You're so athletic, you should think about giving up soccer and trying one of these sports. Now that would be extreme!

Let me hear from you soon because my dad wants to get the tickets as soon as possible. I'll keep my fingers crossed that you're available to join us.

Sincerely,
Rachel (207)

16

EXCITING GAMES

PASSAGE 2

Flying High

With a cold breeze blowing against her face, Kelly Clark takes a deep breath. Then, she balances the front edge of her snowboard on the edge of the halfpipe and pushes off while the audience below cheers for her. A halfpipe is a U-shaped structure made of hard-packed snow. Its steep sides are 18 feet tall.

As a U.S. Olympic gold medal winner, Clark knows how to handle the pressure of competing. The crowd gasps as she sweeps down the slope and shoots up, up, and up into the air on the other side. Before descending, she performs a McTwist, one of her most famous stunts. (108)

Clark looks at ease while she flips and spins in the air. She started taking snowboard lessons in her youth near her Vermont home. She began by learning basic moves, such as leaning in the direction that she wanted her board to turn. The more skills she learned, the more stunts she wanted to attempt.

Now in her twenties, Clark is considered one of the top snowboarders in the world. She is known for her ability to reach great altitudes on the halfpipe. In fact, she often flies 8 or 9 feet into the air. Most snowboarders only reach heights of 5 or 6 feet. (213)

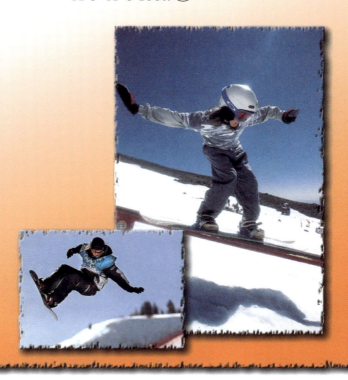

17

Taking a Risk

Last week, my mother told me that she'd won some off-road motorbike lessons to be given at a dirt bike school. She quickly added that she wanted me to have them. My mouth dropped open in response. I've never been athletic, and I don't even drive yet. "Think about it, Greta," she said. "It might be fun." I knew that I was ready for some excitement in my life, but I wasn't sure I was ready for motorbike lessons.

Then, I heard the words, "I'll do it," coming from my mouth.

Before I knew it, I was at the local dirt bike school. I had spent the morning learning about motorbike safety. Now I was putting on my gear, which included gloves, a helmet, boots, and a padded coat and pants. After learning about my bike, I would be ready to take my first ride.

Before long, and after only a few spills, I actually was riding a motorbike across the sandy practice area. It wasn't easy either. I really had to concentrate to manage the hand brake, the foot brake, and four gears all at once. To my astonishment, I was having more fun than I've ever had in my life. I also felt more confident than I had in a long time.

Later, I decided I was ready to attempt the trail. However, our instructor told us it was time for class to end. Now, instead of wondering if I'd enjoy riding a motorbike, I can hardly wait for next week's lesson and the new things I'll learn.

EXCITING GAMES

PASSAGE 4

Freeskiing

Have you ever seen a TV ad that shows a skier zipping down the side of a mountain far away from any marked trails? These ads capture the thrill of an extreme sport called freeskiing.

What Is Freeskiing?

Freeskiing is the most dangerous of all extreme winter sports. The skiers who enjoy this sport start their event at high altitudes. Some of them even use helicopters to get to the beginning of a course. Then, they create their own route as they descend to the bottom of the mountain. Without a marked course, they make their way over boulder fields, sheer cliffs, and steep slopes.

Where Do Freeskiers Ski?

Freeskiers compete in places far away from areas where most skiers go. ⑫¹ The mountain ranges they have been known to attempt include untouched areas in the Rocky Mountains, the Coast Mountains of Canada, and even the Alps.

On What Skills Are Freeskiers Judged?

Freeskiers are judged on the routes they take and on how much they are in control of their runs. They get points for tackling difficult routes. They lose points if they get stuck or lose control.

Who Enjoys Freeskiing?

Freeskiers are extremely athletic skiers. They also must be very familiar with the places they ski. This is because they must make split-second decisions about the best routes to attempt while traveling at top speed. ²²⁷

19

Extreme Sports and the Winter X Games

Some athletes become bored when they play common sports, such as baseball or soccer. Instead, they prefer sports with a lot more action and very few rules. Some of these athletes turn to extreme sports. Extreme sports include activities such as rock climbing, skateboarding, in-line skating, and snowboarding. It's no wonder that extreme sports are popular with youthful athletes.

Extreme sports are called "extreme" for a good reason. They require athletes to push themselves to extreme limits when they compete. The athletes take more risks than they do in other sports. They compete by themselves rather than on a team. They also work hard to develop new abilities. Many of these athletes enjoy making up new stunts.

Each winter, athletes from around the world meet at the Winter X Games. These games were developed by a cable sports network. The first Winter X Games occurred in 1997. Athletes compete in a variety of sports at the games. The events include skiing and snowboarding. Sometimes, new events are added to the games. One of these is called the snowmobile jam. In this event, riders do stunts on snowmobiles. The stunts are similar to those done on dirt bikes.

People from around the world come to watch the Winter X Games. Most would agree that all the events they see have one thing in common. They all are "extremely" exciting.

A Reminder of Summer

Marco watched in silence as the last members of the parade marched down the street and turned the corner. The parade marked the end of summer, and Marco knew what that meant. Soon the weather would get colder.

His days of swimming in the lake and playing in the woods were numbered, not to mention that baseball season soon would end too.

Marco and his grandfather headed back toward the house. Glumly, Marco told Grandpa all the reasons he didn't want summer to end.

"You shouldn't be so worried, Marco," said Grandpa. "You still have some of your summer left. Meanwhile, there are some things you can do to remember summer once it's over."

At the house, Grandpa walked back to his room and returned with a shoe box full of ornaments. He pulled out one that looked like a tiny guitar.

"A musician gave me this guitar when I left Spain. He told me it always could remind me of the Spanish music I knew I would miss so much," he said.

It seemed like Grandpa had a story for every ornament. When he was finished going through them, he handed Marco an ornament that was painted to look like a baseball.

"This will be the beginning of your ornament collection. Maybe you'll collect more as time goes by. For now, though, let's get out to the lake. We might as well enjoy summer while it's still here!" Grandpa said.

Claude Monet's Impressions of His World

Claude Monet once said that he was good at only two things—painting and gardening. Because he is one of the greatest artists of all time, the first thing surely is true.

Monet was among a group of artists who painted in a new way. Instead of working in a studio, he took his paints outdoors. There he paid special attention to the way light fell on the land. He noticed how it glittered on the water. That is what he showed in his paintings. Critics did not like the paintings at first. They said artists such as Monet painted their impressions of the world. That was not what artists had done before.

When he turned 50, Monet realized a lifelong dream. He moved into a house in the French countryside. The estate was surrounded by gardens. (137) Monet worked in the gardens every day. He enjoyed painting pictures of the flowers that he had worked hard to grow.

Among all his subjects, Monet might have loved water scenes most of all. He decided that his home needed a water garden. He and six other gardeners worked steadily for more than a year on this project. They built a beautiful pond surrounded by willow trees and flowers.

Some of Monet's most famous paintings show this pond. These and other paintings of his home tell something about the artist. They give us an idea that what Monet said about himself was true. He indeed was a great painter and a skilled gardener as well. (252)

Word List

polite	discover
interrupt	brilliant
whether	antennae
disgrace	spheres
created	especially
mission	gradually